M000286719

You Can Preach!

Formerly *Lay Speakers Preach!*

John P. Gilbert

Thoughts on Teaching and Learning

Each one of us has a personal and unique learning style. It may be similar to that of others, but if we are able to use a learning style tailored to the way our brain recognizes, stores, and processes information, learning becomes easy and fun, and information is more effectively retained. Think of how you yourself prefer to learn. Perhaps you are a reader. Maybe you learn more easily and efficiently by listening in the form of music, sounds, or by voice. Perhaps you learn best in a 'hands-on' manner. If the teaching method suits your learning style, you can process and adapt any information quickly. Addressing the educational needs of all students during a session may require you to modify your presentation style.

While lecture alone is the least effective means of presenting material, group activity is one of the most effective. Relational activities in small groups, or sometimes in the larger class context, associate students with different learning styles and thereby offer a chance for the teacher to expose the students to multiple avenues of learning. Though some sessions will lend themselves to one or more specific learning styles, the instructor can use a combination to address the needs of the students. As teachers, we need to be creative!

Articles and guidelines concerning multiple intelligences refer to the research of Howard Gardner or the "eight ways of learning." These disciplines can be loosely grouped into three categories, or styles: auditory, visual, or tactile (also known as kinesthetic, as it can involve any form of participatory motion or perceived movement). The chart contains some activity suggestions.

Further help can be obtained in the 'Train the Trainers' section of the *Guidebook for Conference and District Directors* available from Discipleship Resources. You may also find these two books will spark your creativity:

Faithful Guides: Coaching Strategies for Church Leaders by Thomas Hawkins (DR465). Let coaching improve your creative teaching skills.

Always in Rehearsal: The Practice of Worship and the Presence of Children by James H. Ritchie, Jr. (DR427). Ritchie provides a helpful application of the multiple intelligences to the inclusion of all age-levels in corporate worship.

Auditory	Visual	Tactile
class discussion * show and tell * creative rhythms and raps * debate * paraphrase or description * music * songs or rhymes * poetry * storytelling * reading * word games * seminars	charts and graphs * timeline * diagrams * cartoons * bulletin boards * photographs * videos * posters * journal writing * montages and collages * collections	games * simulations * puppets * sculpting * drama * dance * signing * construction * experiments * role-playing * origami * jig-saw puzzles

Welcome

May God's blessings surround you as you explore preaching the gospel of Jesus Christ in a world that needs so desperately to hear the word of God!

The issue facing our world today may not be a lack of preachers. Instead, it may be a lack of preachers who truly proclaim the good news of the gospel and who humble themselves before the awesome task of speaking God's word. Preaching the gospel of Jesus Christ is not a life-and-death matter; it is far more important than that. On the words of preachers often hang the eternal souls of those who hear. It is an awesome task; it is an awesome responsibility; it is an awesome calling and privilege that cannot be ignored.

In The United Methodist Church, we often think of the ordained clergy as those who proclaim the word of God. But in increasing numbers of situations, lay speakers are filling pulpits on temporary and, at times, on permanent bases. Lay speakers are called by God to proclaim God's word but, for myriad reasons, have not or can not prepare themselves formally for the ordained ministry.

To fulfill this need, our General Board of Discipleship has set up standards for lay speakers, including study, deep and sincere prayer, and participation in covenant groups or other kinds of small-group experiences in which faith and theology can be discussed, enriched, and deepened.

Not all lay speakers are called to preach; many serve in a wide variety of other ministries. But almost all lay speakers seek the preparation to be able to preach, should the occasion demand. Perhaps that is the reason you have this book in your hand and are reading these paragraphs. Perhaps you are a lay speaker pondering a call to more extensive preaching; perhaps you are a designated leader preparing to guide a group of lay speakers through this Advanced Course. Perhaps you are an inquirer, wondering if the call you feel—a call to explore the ministry of lay speaking and, ultimately, the call to preach God's word—is truly from God.

For whatever reason you are exploring the ministry of preaching, we pray God's blessings upon you. You are in for an exciting time in the processes of sermon preparation and delivery. But right now, before you do anything else, even before you read another paragraph, pause and pray. Pray for each member of your lay speaking group. Pray for yourself as you prepare to lead this group. Pray that God's presence might be a significant part of all your group sessions. Pray that God will guide you as you seek to carry out the task given you to lead this group of lay speakers.

To the Course Leader

A QUESTION OF OBJECTIVES

In this Advanced Lay Speaking Course on preaching, the list of objectives is brief and precise. Each lay speaker will

- prepare a sermon for a particular congregation;
- deliver that sermon before several other lay speakers in training;
- critique and evaluate her or his own sermon as well as the sermons of several other lay speakers.

This sermon preparation and delivery will be undertaken following a rather precise process outlined in the course text, *Go Preach!: A Primer for Beginning Preachers*.

Of course, any time a group of lay speakers gather, other goals and objectives are recognized and met as each person seeks to strengthen his or her own faith through contact with like-minded Christians. But keep in mind the simple objectives outlined above, for they will guide your preparation.

THE BASIC RESOURCE

The text for this course is *Go Preach!: A Primer for Beginning Preachers*, by John P. Gilbert (Discipleship Resources, 2002). Be sure each member of your group has a copy of the book—or information about how to obtain one—far enough in advance of your first session to read the entire book.

Go Preach! is exactly what the title says—a primer; a beginning; a rudimentary, elementary, start-from-scratch, assume-nothing book about sermon preparation and delivery. For some experienced lay speakers in your group, some of *Go Preach!* will seem old hat. But—and this is important—*Go Preach!* describes a detailed approach for sermon preparation and delivery, a step-by-step process for getting ready to preach, preaching, and evaluating that preaching experience. It will be a guide for those who are preaching for the first time as well as for those who are sharpening their preaching skills.

Some members of your group will argue that they do not want to go through this entire process, that they want to skip some of the steps described in the book, or that they have another way of preparing a sermon. However, for the purposes of this course, insist that all group members follow this procedure rigorously. Remind them that they learned to read using a primer (some of us remember "Run, Spot, run!") and that they had to master that primer before they were ready to move on to more complicated books. Preaching is the same way: Learn to preach by following a simple, step-by-step process; gain experience; then leave the primer behind and dig into some of the more sophisticated books on preaching that are listed in the bibliography.

GETTING READY TO LEAD

Here are some suggestions for conducting your sessions:

- Read *Go Preach!* (called the *Primer* in this course outline) before you begin your preparations. Then read over this entire course outline. Notice especially the suggestions for bringing in a consultant on grammar in Session 3, obtaining extra spaces and equipment for teams in Session 4, and celebrating the Lord's Supper following Session 5. (You may need to invite an ordained elder to conduct this service.)

- Schedule five two-hour sessions. If you have more or less time, adapt these session plans accordingly.

- If possible, schedule the sessions as far apart as possible. For example, one session each week for five weeks is ideal. That schedule gives the members of your group plenty of time to work on assignments. Perhaps the most inconvenient schedule is having all five sessions in one weekend, with little or no time for working on assignments. But because this is often the arrangement for lay speaker training, the session plans can be adapted for a single-weekend arrangement.

- Arrange your meeting space so that participants are seated at tables with plenty of room to work and to write. You will want to have a chalkboard, marker board, or newsprint and markers; an extra table for resources; and a lectern or pulpit.

- Gather a quantity of resources to have available throughout the sessions. Basic resources include

  —a variety of translations of the Bible;

  —several copies of *The United Methodist Hymnal* and *The United Methodist Book of Worship*;

  —a couple Bible dictionaries;

—several Bible atlases;

—a least one exhaustive concordance;

—several Bible commentaries;

—at least one collegiate dictionary;

—at least one thesaurus.

Additional helpful resources include

—a copy of the *Gospel Parallels*;

—*The HarperCollins Bible Pronunciation Guide*;

—one or two histories of the Christian church.

Invite group members to bring some of the tools they use in Bible study and sermon preparation.

A COUPLE OTHER DETAILS

- **Refreshments?** Yes, but keep them simple and make them the kinds of refreshments that group members can get during sessions. Do not interrupt sessions with long refreshment breaks.

- **Nametags?** Again, yes. Use the kinds of nametags that are large enough to be seen easily.

- **Assigned seats?** No. If your group is meeting on other than a single weekend, encourage the members to sit at a different place for each session.

YOUR ROLE AS LEADER

Your role as the group leader is crucial. First, regardless of your experience and background, do not present yourself as the final authority on preaching. Instead, you are a facilitator, someone whose task it is to draw from each participant the best he or she has to offer. Divert direct questions to group discussion. "Should I do this in this sermon?" is best answered by letting the whole group discuss possible responses rather than by you jumping in with the "correct" answer.

Second, each member of your learning group feels that she or he has been called to preach. This means that your role is to encourage, to affirm, to build up. You and the group members are working with people God has summoned. Your group is no place for snickering, chuckling, or laughing at someone's efforts. Use humor in your sessions, but never use humor that is directed at someone's efforts or at an individual.

Your goal is to help provide an experience in which these lay speakers gain confidence in their ability to fulfill their call to preach.

DEAR LAY SPEAKER IN TRAINING,

Greetings in the name of the Lord Jesus Christ! You have enrolled in an exciting adventure for you and for other participants in this Advanced Course, *You Can Preach*. In this course, you will:

> • develop a congregation profile • write a sermon based on lectionary for that congregation • go over that sermon several times • deliver that sermon in full in front of several other participants in this course • evaluate your sermon and several other sermons.

Sound like a big order? It is. The sessions will be fast paced and crammed full. This is not a lecture course; it is a course based on you and your experience as you prepare a sermon and deliver it. Your experience will not make you an accomplished preacher. However, it will give you the confidence to prepare and deliver sermons as you are invited to do so, for it will provide you with a detailed, step-by-step process for sermon construction.

We will meet for five two-hour sessions. These are scheduled for

Dates	Times	Location

The success of this course and the benefit you receive will depend on your willingness to complete the assignments, to participate actively in the small teams, and to arrive on time and stay for the complete session.

Your first assignment is to read the course text, *Go Preach!: A Primer for Beginning Preachers*. Read the book in its entirety. If for some reason you cannot read the entire book, please read the first four chapters before Session 1. But don't just read the book; have a dialogue with it. Underline or highlight portions of the book; make marginal notes; jot down questions, comments, or insights. Realize that this book is not the last word on preaching. Instead, it is the first word, the very first word. That's why it's called a primer.

Please come to each session having completed the assignment given at the last session. Bring your Bible, paper and pencils for note taking, your copy of *Go Preach!*, and your eagerness to participate and to talk about your assignments with others in the group. For the first session, bring a copy of the bulletin from the worship service you attended most recently.

One other crucial element I invite you to bring to each session is the willingness to try. We'll be following a detailed process for sermon preparation and delivery. You may have heard of other approaches to sermon preparation; or if you have preached before, you may have your own process for sermon writing. But please engage totally in and commit to following the process of sermon preparation described in the text. Your experience and the experience of others in the course will be enriched.

Preaching is one of the most holy and awesome tasks that any of us will ever undertake. Therefore, know that I am praying for you as you prepare for this course. I urge you to undergird all of your reading, all of your preparations, all of the work on your assignments with prayer, with constant prayer, with prayer for God's presence and power with you as you respond to God's call to preach.

In God's peace,

SESSION 1:
Worship, Preaching, and the Lectionary

TO THE PARTICIPANT

The purposes of this session are

- to explore each one's call to preach;
- to review the elements of worship in United Methodist congregations;
- to review the Christian Year;
- to recognize the lectionary as a preaching tool.

Preparation for Session 1: Read *Go Preach!: A Primer for Beginning Preachers*, or at least chapters 1 through 4.

If *Go Preach!* is not available until the first session, interview your pastor. Focus on these questions:

- How do you ensure that all the components of the service of worship mesh into a unified experience?
- What, do you believe, is the place and role of the sermon in the order of worship?
- Do you preach from the lectionary? Why or why not?
- What are the lectionary readings for this coming Sunday? Where do you find a list of those readings?

Come to the first session with a Bible, supplies for taking notes, your copy of *Go Preach!*, and a copy of the Sunday worship bulletin from the service of worship you attended most recently.

TO THE LEADER

Before This Session: Contact each participant. The letter on page 4 in this book may be reproduced and sent to your group members. Welcome each one to the training on preaching and go over the schedule of sessions. Encourage each group member to be fully present at each of the five sessions. "Fully present" means arriving on time, remaining until the session is completed, participating in each session, and carrying out all assignments.

Remind each member to obtain the course book, *Go Preach!* (If you have ordered the books for the participants, include the book with your letter.) Encourage each person to read chapters 1 through 4. Invite them to have a dialogue with the text as they read, jotting down questions, comments, ideas, and reactions.

Remind each one to bring a bulletin from the service of worship he or she most recently attended.

Prepare a resource table, including the resources listed on page 3 in this book.

SESSION PLAN

1. Begin the Session (15 minutes)
Open with Scripture, a brief meditation, and prayer. Base your meditation on Isaiah 50:4 or on Matthew 28:18-20.

Welcome the participants and introduce yourself. Here is an opportunity to indicate that you are not the expert on preaching but, instead, a facilitator who will draw insights from each of the group members.

Go over the schedule; that is, on what days and at what times you will be meeting. Remind group members of the basic supplies they will need at each session.

Tell the group about the resource table, point out the locations of restrooms, and make announcements.

2. Explore the Call to Preach (15 minutes)

Ask each group member to turn to someone sitting next to him or her and say, "Tell me about your call to preach the gospel."

After about four or five minutes, ask each person to introduce her or his partner, telling something about that partner's call to preach. When all have been introduced, offer a simple prayer of thanksgiving for the calls to preach the gospel that have been described.

3. United Methodist Worship (20 minutes)

Invite group members to turn to page 3 in *The United Methodist Hymnal* and to call out the major components of a service of worship as you write them on a chalkboard or newsprint. As each component is identified, raise these questions for discussion by the whole group:

- Why is this component in this place in the service of worship?
- How does the placement of this component add to the overall flow of the service of worship?

Divide the group into teams of three. Ask each team to refer to the worship bulletins they brought with them and to discuss these questions:

- How does the service of worship in your congregation reflect these components?
- If the worship service in your congregation is not similar to this outline, how and why does it differ?

Pay attention to the placement of the sermon within each service of worship. What immediately precedes the sermon, and what immediately follows it? Hear reports from a few of the teams. (Hearing reports from every team is not necessary; the benefit of team discussions is within the team, not in the reporting.)

Expect a question about contemporary, informal worship. Outline the contemporary worship sequence on a chalkboard or newsprint. Show that, though the forms of worship may be different, the components are similar. For example, a component might be praising God through a congregational hymn. Forms of this component could include singing from pew hymnals to the accompaniment of a pipe organ or singing to the beat of an onstage rock band and using words projected onto a screen.

4. The Role of the Sermon (15 minutes)

Ask group members to brainstorm as many possible functions or purposes of a sermon as they can. Jot down on a chalkboard or newsprint each idea offered. (Recall the rules of brainstorming: Every idea is allowed, but no editing, commenting, or critiquing is permitted.) If group members have trouble getting started, recall the purpose of a sermon described in the *Primer* (pages 10-12).

Next, form new teams of three (not the same groups as last time). Ask each team to discuss these questions:

- Recall the last sermon you heard. Was it a sermon to inspire, to challenge, to instruct, or to do what?

- What made this sermon that kind of sermon?

- Along with teaching, challenging, and so forth, did this sermon lift up Jesus Christ and proclaim the good news of the gospel? If so, how did this sermon do that? If not, how could this sermon have been changed or altered to proclaim the good news and to lift up Jesus Christ?

5. Break (10 minutes)

6. The Christian Year (20 minutes)
Ask group members to recall as much about the Christian Year as they can from chapter 4 in the *Primer.*

- On what is the Christian Year based?

- When does the Christian Year begin?

- The Christian Year is divided into six periods. What are they? (Refer to page 224 in *The United Methodist Book of Worship* for a quick overview.)

As the six major seasons are added, ask group members to call out special days that occur within each of the seasons. Help group members see, for example, that the Christmas season includes Christmas Eve, Christmas Day, and Epiphany. Included in the Easter season are Easter Sunday, Ascension Day, and Pentecost.

Explain that the Christian Year keeps the church focused on the life of Christ and the life of discipleship. It also ensures that services of worship are devoted to the major elements of our faith. Churches that do not follow the Christian Year may not remember to celebrate such crucial days as Ascension Sunday, Epiphany, All Saints' Day, and Trinity Sunday.

Invite group members to add other special days observed by the church that do not stem directly from the life of Christ and the story of the early church. Suggest national holidays (Independence Day, Memorial Day, Labor Day, Thanksgiving Day, for example), national observances (Mother's Day), and United Methodist and ecumenical special days (World Communion Sunday, Reformation Day, Aldersgate Day).

The Christian Year, with all its special days, is intended to help people remember and relive the life and ministry of Christ, the witness of the early church, and the "great cloud of witnesses" that has shaped who we are and has passed on to us the witness of the Christian faith.

7. The Lectionary (20 minutes)
The *Primer* suggests that beginning preachers use the lectionary in planning and preparing sermons. Divide the group into two debate teams. Ask one team to list all the reasons they can for preaching the lectionary, and the other team to list all the reasons they can for ignoring the lectionary and preaching whatever one chooses.

Assign a spokesperson for each team. Give each spokesperson two minutes to make an initial argument and one minute to respond to the other spokesperson's arguments. Expect some humor.

Discuss the reason for three lections and a psalm in each week's lectionary. Remind the group members that using all four Scriptures in a sermon is not always necessary; some of the lections can be used within the service in other ways. Ask group members to list some of those ways. (Refer to chapter 4 in the *Primer*, if necessary.)

Invite questions and comments regarding the lectionary and its use. Distribute copies of *The United Methodist Book of Worship*, and call the group's attention to pages 227 and following. Point out the three years (A, B, C), noting that each year begins with Advent. Also point out some of the special days for which lections are supplied (for example, the days of Holy Week, on page 231).

Ask if the idea of the lectionary is new to any in the group. Acknowledge that some pastors do not use the lectionary and do not follow the Christian Year. Emphasize again that preaching from the lectionary is freeing, not shackling, for the beginning preacher; it is liberating, not restricting.

8. Make Assignments (5 minutes)

For the next session, ask each group member to

1. read chapters 5, 6, and 7 in the *Primer*;

2. identify the lectionary readings for the Sunday immediately following your next session;

3. come to the next session with these items in hand:

   - the point of a sermon based on the lections for the Sunday immediately following your next session (see chapter 5);

   - a profile of a congregation (see chapter 6);

   - three copies of an outline of a sermon based on the lections and designed for the congregation profiled.

Close this time together with a prayer of thanksgiving for the call to preach, a prayer of thanksgiving for each member of the group, and a prayer seeking God's guidance as the group begins the task of sermon preparation.

SESSION 2:
Preparing a Sermon

TO THE PARTICIPANT

The purpose of this session is

- to critique the participants' first attempts at choosing a sermon topic, preparing a profile of the congregation, and developing a sermon outline.

Preparation for Session 2: Read chapters 5, 6, and 7 in *Go Preach!: A Primer for Beginning Preachers.*

Choose a single main point for a sermon using the lectionary Scriptures for the Sunday immediately following the date of Session 2. Write a profile of the congregation and a sermon outline.

TO THE LEADER

You and the group will spend most of this session examining the central points and outlines the group members have built around one or more of the lections for the coming week and their profiles of the congregation. If your schedule is such that group members did not have time to complete these assignments (for example, if you are completing this course over a weekend), devote the first thirty minutes of the session to this individual work. Seek permission to use spaces in your meeting building in addition to your meeting room—Sunday school classrooms, the fellowship hall, or some other spaces—so that the group members can work individually and quietly.

Even if your sessions have been spread out over several weeks, allow about fifteen minutes at the beginning of the session so that group members who have not completed their assignments may do so. Those who have completed their assignments can use this time to review the three chapters in the *Primer* and to polish their work.

SESSION PLAN

1. Worship and Introduction (15 minutes)
Begin with a brief meditation and prayer built around a passage of Scripture to serve as a model for the group.

Next, post the three lections and psalm for the coming Sunday, the Scriptures on which your group members are building sermons. Make brief comments on these lectionary Scriptures, such as providing some background on passages that are illuminated by context. Tell the group members where you got this background—commentary, atlas, dictionary, and so forth. If possible, show them the actual materials you used.

2. The Point of the Sermon (25 minutes)
Form teams of three (not the same groups as the last session). Give each team this assignment:

> Tell your team the central point or idea you found in these lectionary readings. Identify that point in a single sentence. Then explain how you came to that point from these lections.

Encourage the other team members to quiz the presenter about her or his main point. Display these sample questions to get them started in the right direction.

- How does this point proclaim the good news?
- How does this point glorify Jesus Christ?
- Does this point emerge from the Scripture readings, or is this point being read back into the Scripture?
- And here's a tough one: If the point emerges primarily from one reading, is it consistent with the main points of the other readings? In what ways?

Warning: Do not let anyone challenge a point to the extent of saying that a point is wrong, incorrect, or not grounded in the Scriptures. One of the major emphases of this exercise is to demonstrate how several different points can emerge from one set of lections.

As the teams report on their sermon points, jot them down on the chalkboard or newsprint. *Note:* Do most come from the Gospel reading? from a combination of all four lectionary Scriptures? from the Old Testament reading?

If some reports include several points in a single sermon, refer to the *Primer* for the importance of single-point sermons (pages 57-58). If someone suggests a two- or three-point sermon, push that person to focus on a single point.

3. Profiles of the Congregation (25 minutes)
Move to the task of profiling the congregation for whom this sermon will be preached.

- What kinds of information about the congregation were easy to obtain? What kinds were difficult?
- Who are the key people who can provide information about your own congregation?

(Remember, information is not gossip about individuals; it is a demographic snapshot of the congregation.)

Next, ask the group to form new teams of three. Ask each team member to tell the other two members about her or his profile. Encourage the two listeners in each team to raise questions about each profile and to indicate some of the kinds of information that are not included in the profile but which might be helpful for sermon preparation. Recognize, of course, that you will never have all the information you need to customize a sermon precisely for a specific congregation. If time permits, the listeners might ask this question: "If some of the information you gathered were just the opposite, how would your sermon be different?" (For example, if the sermon is for a small-membership congregation of elderly people, how might the same sermon be recast for a large-membership congregation of children, youth, and young adults?)

Reassemble. Ask: "What kinds of information about a congregation are essential in planning a sermon?" List these on the chalkboard or newsprint. Then encourage the group to determine which three or four pieces of information are central to planning a sermon for a specific congregation. Challenge the group members to gather this data before preaching any sermon.

4. Break (10 minutes)

5. Sermon Outlines (35 minutes)
Now move to discussing sermon outlines. Before returning to new teams of three, remind the group members of these factors about sermon outlines:

- First, although some schoolteachers would object to this, no hard and fast rules dictate an outline's skeleton. That is, you can start with Roman numerals or capital letters; subpoints can be regular numerals or bullets. Do not get hung up on the form and skeleton.
- Second, a single word is not sufficient for a point or a subpoint in an outline. A simple phrase or sentence that incorporates that word is necessary.
- Third, an outline should be sufficiently detailed so that a person reading it could grasp both the central point of the sermon and the arguments used to arrive at that central point.

Form new teams of three to talk about the outlines. If the participants have not brought copies for their small team, let them make copies now, if possible.

As team members review one another's outlines, they should be able to follow the development of each sermon. But as this may be the first attempt many of your group members have made at outlining a sermon, encourage group members not to expect perfection from one another or from themselves. This is a shared learning opportunity—no grades, no evaluations, no kudos or criticisms, only mutual support. Encourage team members to reexamine and be willing to revise their outlines in the light of insights gained from these discussions.

Reassemble as a whole group and do a review. Raise questions such as these:

- What did you find easy about preparing an outline, and what did you find difficult? Why, do you think, is this so?
- Why is an outline necessary in sermon preparation? Why not just go from the central point to the preparation of the manuscript?

Refer to the *Primer* for some preliminary answers to these questions. You might indicate that sometimes with experience comes less dependence on an outline, but even the best and most experienced preachers often outline their sermons prior to preparing the manuscript.

6. Assignments and Worship (10 minutes)

Make assignments for the next session:

- Encourage group members to read chapters 8, 9, and 10 before the next session.
- Invite group members to reexamine their outlines based on insights gained through their group evaluations and then to write a first draft of a sermon.

Ask for a volunteer to open the next session with a three-minute devotional. Remind this volunteer that she or he should go through the same process of studying the Scriptures, determining the central point, outlining the devotional, and preparing a manuscript as if she or he were delivering a twenty-minute sermon. Also, the volunteer must bear in mind the particular congregation (the group members) for whom this devotional is being offered.

Close this session with a word of affirmation for the hard work group members did in preparation for this session and for their active participation in the teams of three. Close with a prayer of thanksgiving for the group members and for their commitment to proclaiming the gospel of Jesus Christ.

SESSION 3:
Perfecting the Sermon

TO THE PARTICIPANT

The purposes of this session are

- to understand the need for good grammar, style, and word selection;
- to consider the use, and misuse, of humor in the pulpit;
- to recognize the importance of practice.

Preparation for Session 3: Read chapters 8, 9, and 10 in *Go Preach!: A Primer for Beginning Preachers*. Write a first draft of a sermon based on responses to your outline in Session 2.

TO THE LEADER

Invite an English teacher to serve as a resource person on grammar and word choice and to make a brief presentation on the five or six most common grammatical errors made in spoken English. If you cannot recruit an English teacher, interview an English teacher (or other person familiar with language usage). Talk about some of the common errors in everyday speech. Discuss words that are frequently misused, phrases that are grammatically misleading, and sentence structures that are too complex to be understood easily. Be prepared to report to the group.

Expect some grumbling. A few may argue that correct grammar and proper word choice is not important; the message of the gospel is. But because the message of the gospel is so important, it needs to be delivered in precise and clear English.

Be sure the group understands that clear, precise English does not mean the use of unfamiliar words or complex sentence structures. Indeed, the gospel is best presented in simple, clear sentences. Because the gospel is best presented in simple sentences with a simple vocabulary, those sentences must be grammatically correct.

SESSION PLAN

1. Opening Worship (5 minutes)
Open with the brief meditation planned by the volunteer from the last session. (Warn this person ahead of time that you will be timing the meditation. The ability to speak to a specific time parameter is an important skill to acquire, so do not let this person ramble on into a twenty-minute sermon.) Do not involve the group in critiquing the meditation, but take time at the conclusion of the session to give your responses privately.

2. Grammar Is Important (20 minutes)
Invite the English teacher to make a short presentation, or report on your interview with an English teacher or an editor. Emphasize the importance of good grammar and sentence construction, good choice of words, and careful attention to pronunciation. If time permits, consider some examples of poor grammar such as these:

- Each person has their own way of doing it. (*Their* should be *his or her*.)
- He had took the materials home. (Use either *He took* or *He had taken*.)

- The purpose of these verses are to show a new way to live. (*Purpose* is the subject. *Are* should be *is*.)

- Neither James nor John could not understand what Jesus was saying. (Delete the word *not*.)

- After the mother and daughter heard Jesus, she praised God. (*She* should be *they*.)

3. Check and Recheck (25 minutes)

Divide the group into pairs, preferably people who do not know each other well. Ask each pair to exchange the first page of their sermon manuscripts. Have them read that page of each other's manuscript and jot down any concerns about grammar, sentence structure, or word choice. Explain that the task is not to correct each other's manuscript page but, rather, to call into question those points about which there may be some uncertainty. After a few minutes, have them discuss that page with his or her partner. If neither partner is sure about a grammatical construction or word choice, both of them should make a note of it and be ready to discuss it with the whole group.

Hear a report from some of the pairs. Emphasize that when they are reporting they shouldn't say, "He was wrong in writing it this way" or "She used the wrong word here." Instead, they should cite an example of a questionable grammatical point and let the whole group discuss that point. Remind group members that hearing something all the time does not make it right.

Because this time spent on grammar and word choice may be a bit intimidating or threatening, remind the group of the two examples that open chapter 8 in the *Primer*. Then ask group members to name examples of bad grammar, poor word choice, or serious mispronunciations they have heard in sermons (no names or places, just the stories).

4. Break (10 minutes)

5. Laughing All the Way (30 minutes)

Chapter 9 in the *Primer* deals with the use of humor and stories within a sermon. Divide your group into teams of five or six people. Ask the members of each team to cluster their chairs so that they can all hear comfortably as they discuss the use of humor in sermons using questions such as these:

- Give some examples and illustrations of humor used effectively in sermons.

- How did the humor add to making the point?

- How did it contribute to the proclamation of the good news of the gospel?

After several people have spoken, pose these questions:

- Who or what was the target of the humor?

- Was this humor offensive to anyone in any way?

Next, ask team members to name examples of humor used ineffectively or inappropriately in a sermon. Have them think of categories here. For example, they may cite illustrations of humor that were used just for the sake of the humor, with no relevance to the sermon point. Or they may name humor that indirectly or slyly insulted or put down people or groups of people. Some may cite examples of humor that were clearly inappropriate. What made these examples inappropriate? (Talk about categories;

do not repeat the offensive jokes.)

Remind team members that such often-heard comments as "I meant it as a joke," "She just can't take a joke," or "Everybody kids about that" are never excuses for hurtful humor from the pulpit.

Ask each team to make a list of types of humor that are never appropriate in a sermon. The list should include humor that negatively stereotypes any group of people, that is dependent on embarrassing a family member ("You won't believe what my teenager did the other day!"), or that even hints at containing a double-entendre; that is, humor that borders on being off-color.

Finally, ask the teams to discuss humor that may have a place in a sermon (such as humor that recognizes our human foibles), that is based on innocent puns (often used in the Hebrew Bible), or that is directed at self, as long as no others are laughed at while laughing at one's self.

Hear reports from some of the teams. Then work as a total group to develop a consensus list of five rules for using humor in sermons. Remember insights from the *Primer*, from team discussions, and from experience.

6. Practice Helps Make Perfect (20 minutes)

Chapter 10 in the *Primer* looks at some final readings of the sermon and then considers practicing or rehearsing the sermon. One suggestion in chapter 10 is that the preacher read one page of the sermon aloud and then describe what comes next in the sermon as a way of fixing the sequence of the sermon in his or her mind.

Divide into pairs again (different pairs than used earlier). Suggest that pairs find quiet places to work. Ask one person in each pair to read the first page of her or his sermon aloud for her or his partner and then to put the manuscript down and describe what comes next. The presenter may be able to describe the major subpoints that follow without referring to the manuscript or outline. But remind your group members that all of them may not be able to do this. This inability to recall the sequence of subpoints is not unusual.

After about ten minutes, reassemble and respond to any questions. Discuss questions such as these:

- The *Primer* describes several ways to practice a sermon. Which of these is most practical for you?
- What are the benefits of practicing or rehearsing a sermon before delivering it?
- What are some of the drawbacks of practicing?
- The *Primer* describes leaving some of the best sermons in the car. What does this mean?
- How can one avoid overpracticing?
- How does a preacher know when she or he has practiced enough?

7. Assignments and Closing Prayer (10 minutes)

Assign chapters 11 and 12 in the *Primer*, and tell group members to prepare to deliver their sermons. They will decide if they will use their manuscripts, outlines, or cards as they deliver their sermons.

Ask for a volunteer to begin your next session with a three-minute devotional.

Close the session with a prayer of thanksgiving for the privilege of proclaiming the gospel of Jesus Christ.

SESSION 4:
Delivering the Sermon

TO THE PARTICIPANT

The purpose of this session is

• to hear and respond to the participants' sermons.

Preparation for Session 4: Read chapters 11 and 12 in *Go Preach!: A Primer for Beginning Preachers*. Finish preparations for preaching your sermon.

TO THE LEADER

Most of this session will be devoted to hearing group members' sermons. Make arrangements for as many meeting spaces as you have teams. Provide a lectern or pulpit (a simple music stand may suffice in some cases) and sufficient chairs for the remainder of the team.

Divide your group into teams of four. You may want to assign groups to ensure that people do not choose teams with members they have been with several times before.

Make for each participant four photocopies of the response form on page 15 in this book.

SESSION PLAN

1. Opening Worship (5 minutes)

Open this session with a brief meditation offered by a group member. Do not critique this meditation; simply acknowledge it and thank

the presenter. You may wish to speak with the meditation presenter following the session if you have suggestions for improvement.

2. Assignment for the Session (5 minutes)

Describe for your group members the tasks for this session:

• The class will be divided into teams of four.

• Each team will be assigned a room or a space. Each space is equipped with chairs and with a lectern, pulpit, or music stand.

• Each member of a team will preach her or his entire sermon to the other three team members.

—The sermon will begin with the reading of one or more passages of Scripture and end with an invitation or a challenge that is appropriate to the sermon.

—One of the three listeners for each sermon will be a timekeeper. No sermon, including Scripture and invitation, is to run more than twenty minutes.

—Each sermon will be followed by five minutes of discussion that will focus on some of the topics throughout this course.

—Each team member (including the preacher) will be given a response form to complete following each sermon. Do not write responses as a sermon is being delivered, as this is discourteous.

Say: "For many of you, this is the first full sermon you have ever preached. Do not expect perfection of yourself or of those on your team. The discussion period following each sermon is not intended to tell you what you did wrong but to be an enriching experience for the whole team. The response sheets will assist in this discussion, which is not an evaluation or a critique, not a judgment on the sermon or the presenter, not a challenge to someone's call to preach. It is a learning experience and an opportunity for all on the team.

"I will be circulating among the teams to listen to some bits of some of the sermons. Please do not let my coming and going distract you if you are preaching.

"Do you have any questions before we begin?

"All right. These are the teams (*read the names*). The first group will go to room ___, the second group to room ___ (*and so on*). Pick up your response sheets as you go to your team meeting room. We will return to this room for a wrap-up in one hour and forty minutes."

3. Go Preach (100 minutes)
Be sure that each group member has four response sheets (one for each sermon she or he will hear and one for evaluating her or his own sermon). Verify the time schedule, but do your best to avoid asking group members to cut their sermons short. The purpose of this activity is to deliver the entire sermon as written and prepared.

Do a quick time check to be sure that each team is beginning its last sermon about thirty-five minutes before your time for adjournment.

4. Follow-up and Assignments (10 minutes)
Call the teams back together in the regular meeting room with about ten to fifteen minutes remaining in the session time.

Invite any group member to tell about her or his experience in preaching a sermon and in listening carefully (and critically) to another's sermon. Do not expect responses from everyone, but take the time to hear two or three new insights that emerged as a result of this sermon delivery.

Make assignments for the next session. Group members are to read chapters 13, 14, and 15 in the *Primer* and to come with any questions, concerns, ideas, or insights about sermon preparation and delivery that they may have. Additionally, ask group members to evaluate their own sermons using some of the suggestions in chapter 13 in the *Primer*. As you have for the last two sessions, ask a volunteer to prepare an opening Scripture passage, devotional, and prayer for your next session.

SESSION 5:
Listening and Dealing with Resistance

TO THE PARTICIPANT

The purposes of this session are

- to explore appropriate responses to comments from the congregation;
- to learn how to create and use a sermon file;
- to consider speaking on special occasions.

Preparation for Session 5: Read chapters 13, 14, and 15 in *Go Preach!: A Primer for Beginning Preachers*. Evaluate your own sermon using suggestions from chapter 13.

TO THE LEADER / SESSION PLAN

1. Opening Worship (5 minutes)
Invite the volunteer to offer his or her opening devotional. Acknowledge the presentation, thank the presenter, and remind the group members that they will be called on often to present short meditations and devotionals for different kinds of occasions.

2. Review of the Last Session (20 minutes)
Spend a few moments reviewing your last session, when each group member delivered her or his sermon. Ask:

- How do you think preaching to three friends in this setting was similar to and different from preaching in front of a congregation of friends or of strangers?
- As you reflected on your sermon and some of the responses to it, what additional insights into sermon preparation and delivery have you discovered?

Hint: Do not be surprised by any questions. Also, do not feel that you must answer every question as the authoritative expert on the subject of preaching. Respond to questions out of your own experiences or by asking the group members what their responses to the questions might be. Many questions will have no right or wrong answers. In some cases, the most appropriate answer may be, "Try it. If it works for you, great!"

Expect someone to ask if the process outlined in the *Primer* must be followed with every sermon and, indeed, with every meditation or devotional. Emphasize that the answer is yes. In time, almost every preacher develops some shortcuts. But the process described in the *Primer* must be mastered by a beginning preacher before shortcuts are possible. Affirm with the group members that the sermon preparation process is difficult, time consuming, detailed, complicated, and exhaustive. But affirm with—or for—the group members that preaching a sermon is one of the most important things they will ever do. Consequently, sermon preparation and delivery demands the best each person has to give. Remind the group members that refusing an opportunity to preach due to lack of preparation time is far better than accepting an invitation to preach and arriving at the appointed day ill-prepared and poorly equipped to deliver the sermon.

3. "Fine Message, Preacher!" (20 minutes)
Try some role-play. Ask one group member to

play the part of a guest preacher who has just completed a service of worship and is standing at the door of the sanctuary. Ask five or six other group members to play the parts of members of the congregation who are filing out past the preacher. Let each church member greet the preacher using a variety of comments often heard following a sermon. Let one person gush over a great sermon, another mumble "Good morning" and little else, a third challenge the preacher on several points, and so on. Observe the preacher's responses. How does she or he react to each kind of greeting—or lack of greeting? What kinds of physical contact does the preacher make, especially in view of the contact that some of the worshipers make with him or her?

Ask group members to quickly review salient parts of chapter 13 in the *Primer*. Then develop a consensus list of guidelines for accepting and reacting to the comments of worshipers following a sermon and service of worship.

Raise this question for general comment: "If you cannot always trust the comments you hear from members of the congregation, who can you trust to give you an honest and genuine evaluation of the sermon?" Recall that the *Primer* suggests not laying this responsibility on a spouse or family member. Ask, "Why not?"

4. Break (10 minutes)

5. Review Learnings (10 minutes)
Direct group members to rejoin the preaching teams from the last session.

Ask each member of each team to review quickly for the other team members the evaluation she or he made of her or his own sermon by using some of the suggestions in chapter 13 in the *Primer*. Focus on learnings from this evaluation process:

- What insights into sermon preparation and delivery emerged from this self-evaluation process?
- And here's a tough question: Did the self-evaluation process concur with the comments and reactions received following the delivery of the sermon at the last session?

That second question has a point: Although a sermon presents a case or makes an argument, it is not to be defended following its delivery. A sermon must stand on its own as it is delivered. Seldom if ever does the preacher have an opportunity to clarify or supplement a sermon; never does a preacher have the right to defend (clarify and explain, perhaps, but not defend) one of her or his sermons. A preacher may quite justifiably dig in his or her heels about a theological point or about a justice and righteousness stance. Help group members understand that arguing with listeners about the merits and presentation of a sermon is fraught with failure.

6. The Sermon File (20 minutes)
Discuss the sermon file. The *Primer* makes suggestions about what to save and how to save it. Go over these briefly, especially the four cross-reference identifications on a sermon folder. Pose this question: "Why is saving the revised profile of the congregation important?" Push for in-depth answers, preferably with illustrations.

Raise this question for general discussion: "The *Primer* suggests that we never preach the same sermon twice (unless we preach it two or more times on the same day, as in a multiple-point charge or in a church with more than one Sunday service of worship). Is this realistic? And if this is realistic, why save old sermons and profiles of the congregation?"

Help the group members understand the difference between lifting an old sermon out of the file and preaching it just as it was when first written and referring to the sermon file for illustrations, ideas, insights, and devices that communicated effectively and helped make a sermon come alive. Remind them that using parts of former sermons is not simply a cut-and-paste task. Instead, those elements always need to be reworked, revised, and reintegrated into the new sermon under construction. Also, remind group members that their after-sermon comments and notes on the manuscript may be of greater value than the actual sermon.

Recall some of your own experiences here. Tell about times when you pulled a sermon from the barrel and tried to get it to work again. Then, on the opposite side of the coin, tell about some of your own experiences of finding insights, ideas, and nuances in former sermons that helped to illuminate and bring to life a sermon currently under construction.

7. Speaking on Special Occasions (20 minutes)

Refer group members to chapter 15 in the *Primer*. Ask how many of them have been invited to speak a few words on a special occasion, such as a funeral. Then ask the group to form teams of three to discuss the following:

- Describe a time when you heard what you believed was a good, positive, uplifting funeral sermon or words by a family member or friend. What made what was said effective? What was the focus of what was said—the person's life, the promises of the gospel, or both?

- Describe a funeral sermon that you believed to be inappropriate. Why was this so? (Remember that funeral customs vary widely across the nation. What is considered appropriate in some parts of the country may seem inappropriate in other regions.)

Hear brief reports from some of the teams, and respond to any questions that may be raised.

Now ask the teams to discuss this set of questions:

- If you were asked to prepare a devotional to open a meeting of your congregation's administrative council, what would you choose as your focus?

- If you were asked to open a meeting of the United Methodist Women or the United Methodist Men with a devotional, what would be your central point?

- If you were invited to open a meeting of a civic club or organization with a devotional, what questions would you raise before you could do so?

Again, hear reports from some of the teams, and respond as a whole group to any questions. Emphasize that preparing a five-minute meditation or devotional may be as difficult as preparing a sermon. A brief devotional demands that the presenter make her or his point concisely, clearly, and directly. Doing so in three minutes may pose difficulties for some people.

8. Closing and Worship (15 minutes)

Conclude this session by recalling some of the things learned as a result of your experience in this course. Thank the group for these learnings. Congratulate members of the group on their participation throughout the sessions, and challenge them to continue to respond to the call to proclaim the good news of the gospel and to lift up Christ Jesus as Lord and Savior.

If arrangements have been made to celebrate the sacrament of the Lord's Supper, invite the group members to prepare themselves to worship and to expect Christ's presence in the bread and the cup.

If you are not going to celebrate the Lord's Supper, close with sentence prayers of thanksgiving for all those in the group.

SERMON RESPONSE

Preacher: _____   Sermon Title: _____

Sermon Text or Texts: _____

Single Main Point of Sermon: _____

Sermon Construction

USE OF THE LECTIONS

Integrity of the sermon
(How true was the sermon to the texts?)

———————————————————

———————————————————

———————————————————

Logical flow and development

———————————————————

———————————————————

———————————————————

When/how was the central point
introduced?

———————————————————

———————————————————

———————————————————

When/how was the central point
reinforced?

———————————————————

———————————————————

———————————————————

Use of illustrations and humor, if applicable

———————————————————

———————————————————

———————————————————

Choice of words

———————————————————

———————————————————

———————————————————

SENTENCE STRUCTURE
Overall interest level (Did this sermon
hold my interest? Why or why not?)

———————————————————

———————————————————

———————————————————

———————————————————

Complete this sentence stem: I could
have understood the main point of the
sermon easier and more effectively if…

———————————————————

———————————————————

———————————————————

(This sheet may be duplicated for use in Lay Speakers' courses. © 2002 Discipleship Resources.)